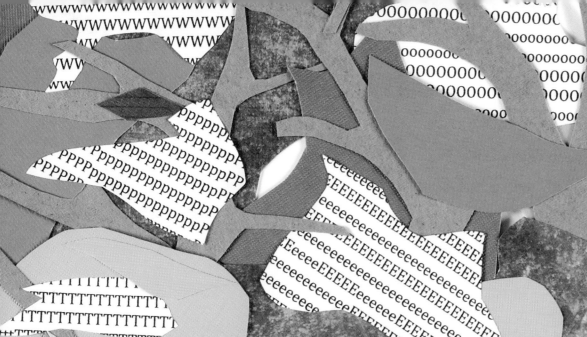

Amazon
Alphabet

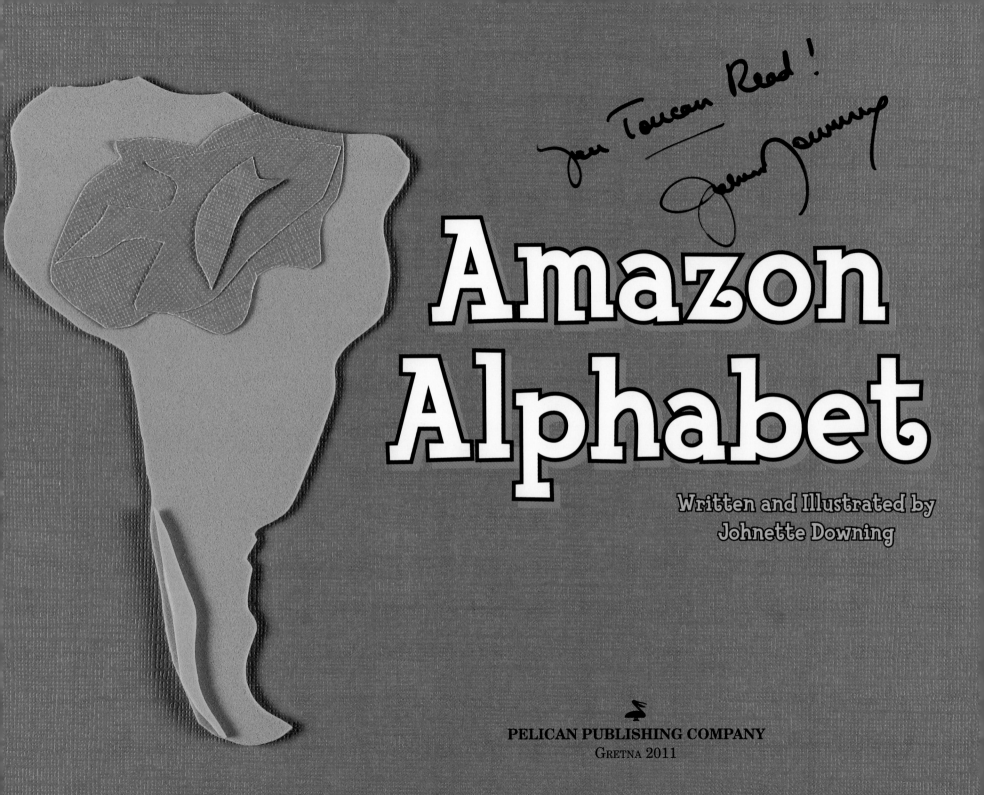

You Toucan Read !
Johnette Downing

Amazon Alphabet

Written and Illustrated by
Johnette Downing

PELICAN PUBLISHING COMPANY
Gretna 2011

The word "Pelican" and the depiction of a pelican are trademarks
of Pelican Publishing Company, Inc., and are registered in the
U.S. Patent and Trademark Office.

Library of Congress Cataloging-in-Publication Data

Downing, Johnette.
  Amazon alphabet / written and illustrated by Johnette Downing.
    p. cm.
  ISBN 978-1-58980-879-9 (hardcover : alk. paper) 1. Animals—Amazon
River Region—Juvenile literature. 2. Rain forests—Amazon River Region—
Juvenile literature. 3. Amazon River—Juvenile literature. 4. Amazon River
Region—Juvenile literature. 5. English language—Alphabet—Juvenile litera-
ture. 6. Alphabet books. I. Title.
  QL235.D69 2011
  591.981'1—dc22

                                  2010029022

Printed in China
Published by Pelican Publishing Company, Inc.
1000 Burmaster Street, Gretna, Louisiana 70053

The Amazon River is the largest river system in the world and runs through nine South American countries: Brazil, Bolivia, Peru, Ecuador, Colombia, Venezuela, Guyana, French Guiana, and Suriname.

A is for Amazon.

B

B is for boa constrictor.

Emerald tree boa constrictors are camouflaged to blend in with the forest and spend most of their lives coiled around tree branches.

C is for caiman.

The black caiman is the largest member of the alligator family in the Americas and the largest predator in the Amazon Basin.

Pink dolphins live in rivers and have 40 percent more brain capacity than humans.

D is for dolphin.

E is for electric eel.

The electric eel is not an eel but a fish, and it shocks its prey with an electric charge.

Poison dart frogs
are very toxic. Their
brilliant colors warn
predators to keep
away.

F is for frog.

G is for grasshopper.

The grasshopper is an insect that rubs its long hind legs together to make a chirping sound.

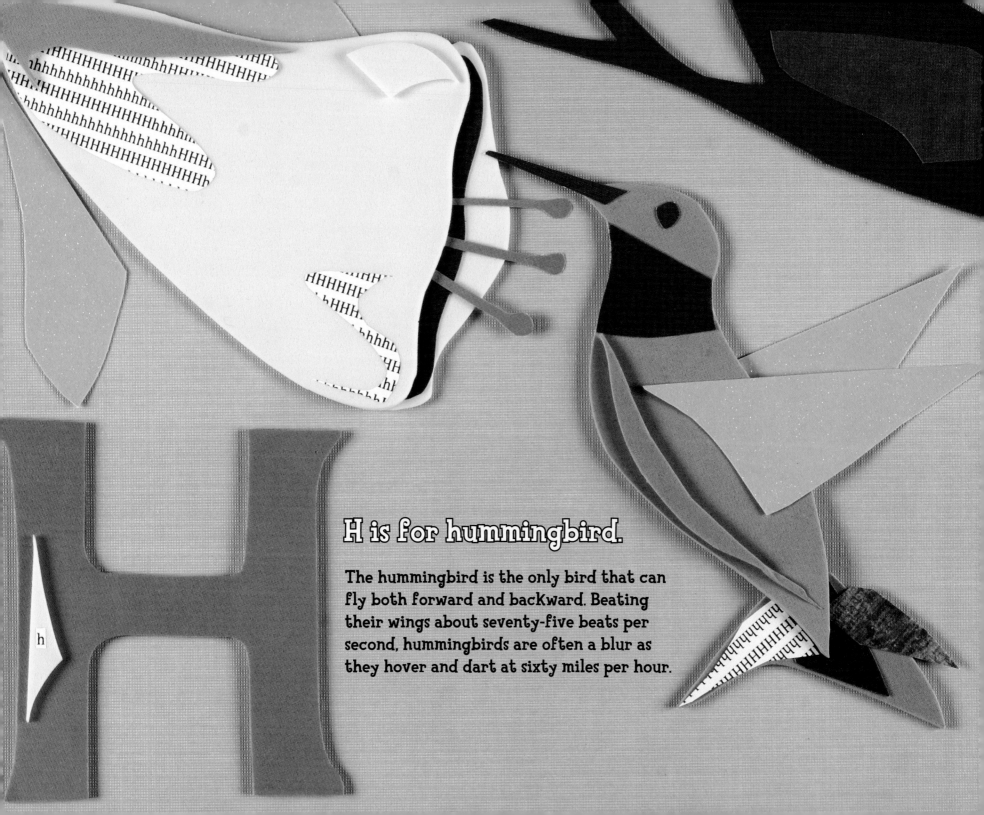

H is for hummingbird.

The hummingbird is the only bird that can fly both forward and backward. Beating their wings about seventy-five beats per second, hummingbirds are often a blur as they hover and dart at sixty miles per hour.

I is for iguana.

Though the green iguanas are good swimmers, they live in the forest canopy, high in the trees, to bask in the sun.

J is for jaguar.

Jaguars are the largest felines in the Western Hemisphere. Their coats are covered in clusters of spots for camouflage.

K is for Katydid.

Katydids belong to the grasshopper family and sing at night. Their song sounds like "Katy did; Katy didn't."

L is for leafcutter ant.

Leafcutter ants chew off bits of
leaves and carry them home to grow
a fungus they like to eat.

The manatee is the Amazon's largest marine
mammal and is more closely related to the
elephant than to other marine animals.
It lives in both salt and fresh water.

M is for manatee.

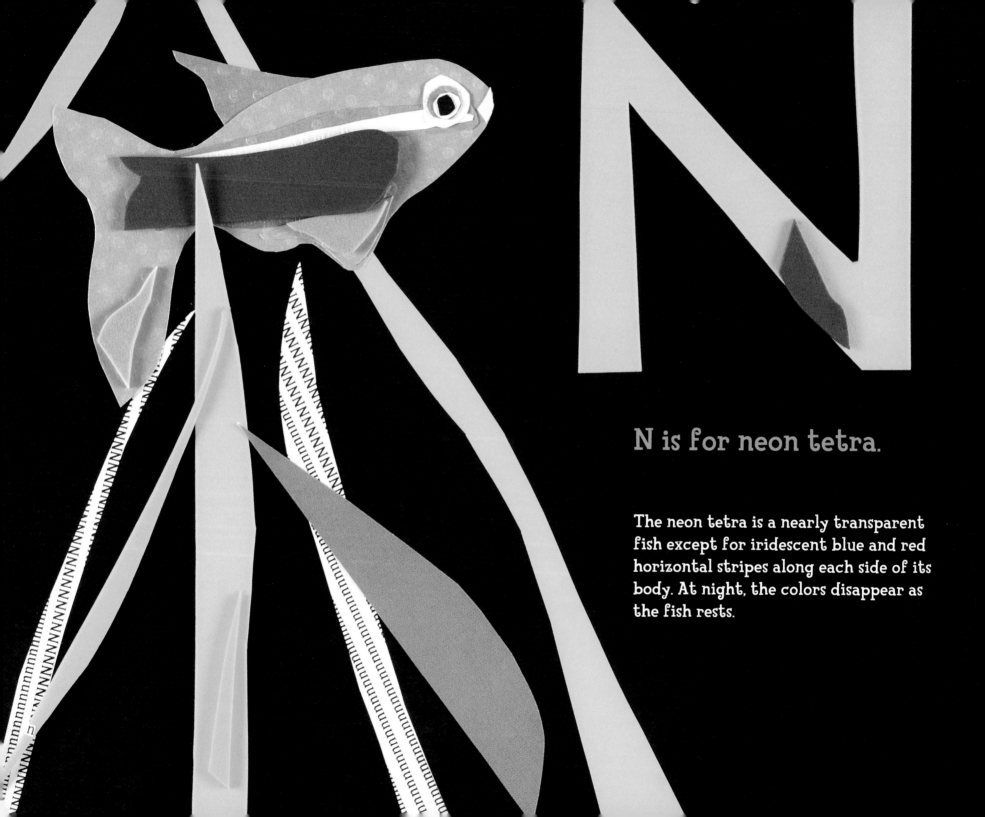

N is for neon tetra.

The neon tetra is a nearly transparent fish except for iridescent blue and red horizontal stripes along each side of its body. At night, the colors disappear as the fish rests.

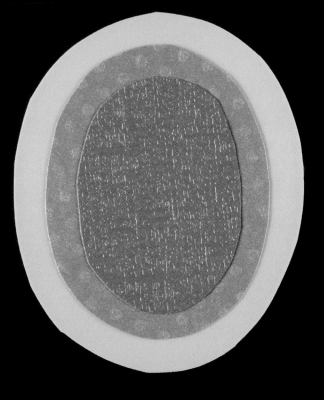

O is for ocelot.

Ocelots are good runners, swimmers, and climbers. They can climb down trees backward.

P is for piranha.

Piranhas travel in large schools for protection and are known for their razor-sharp teeth and powerful jaws.

Q is for quetzal.

These brightly colored birds are poor flyers. The male, with tail feathers up to three feet long, helps incubate the eggs and feed the hatchlings.

R

R is for rainforest.

The Amazon rainforest is called the "Lungs of the Planet" because it produces about 20 percent of the Earth's oxygen. The largest rainforest in the world, it consists of four forest layers: emergent, canopy, understory, and forest floor.

S is for sloth.

Three-toed sloths are the slowest mammals on Earth and sleep between fifteen and eighteen hours per day.

T is for toucan.

The toucan is known for its large,
brightly colored beak. Though a
toucan's beak looks heavy, it is
actually hollow.

U is for umbrellabird.

Umbrellabirds are known for the
retractable umbrella-like crests
on their heads and long, feathered
wattles on their throats.

V is for vampire bat.

The bat is the only flying mammal on Earth. The vampire bat uses echolocation (a method of finding objects using reflected sound) to locate its prey and then it drinks its blood.

W is for woolly monkey.

Woolly monkeys are among the largest monkeys in the Amazon Basin. They communicate with each other by using facial expressions and calls.

X

X is for x-ray fish.

X-ray fish are small, adaptable fish with transparent bodies. Their internal organs are visible.

Y is for yapok.

The yapok or water opossum has webbed hind feet and is the only existing aquatic marsupial (a mammal with a distinctive pouch to carry its young).

Z is for zoologist,

and that's who studies animals
in the Amazon alphabet!

RAINFOREST FUN FACTS

1. The Amazon rainforest is a tropical forest, with a constant temperature of seventy-five to eighty degrees, located along the Equator in South America. It is called a "rainforest" because it has large trees, plenty of sunlight, and rains every day, approximately eighty inches of rain per year.

2. Covering only about 2 percent of the Earth's surface, tropical rainforests are home to more than half the world's species of plants, animals, and insects, many of which can only survive in the rainforest.

3. The Amazon is home to tribal people who rely on the rainforest for food, shelter, and medicines.

4. At least 80 percent of the world's diet originated in tropical rainforests, including at least three thousand types of fruits, such as bananas, mangos, and oranges.

5. Approximately one-fifth of the world's fresh water is in the Amazon Basin.

6. Tropical rainforests are vital to stabilizing the Earth's ecosystem by exchanging water and energy with the atmosphere, continuously recycling carbon dioxide into oxygen, and recycling and cleaning water.

7. Trees and plants serve as anchors to help protect against soil erosion, drought, and flood. Without trees and plants, the soil washes into and pollutes rivers.

RAINFOREST CONSERVATION

Rainforests are slowly disappearing across the globe because humans are cutting down the trees to build houses, buildings, and furniture and to clear land for roads and cattle farms. As the rainforests vanish, the animals and plants that live in them also vanish. However, if left intact and managed properly, rainforests have much more economic and ecological value providing the world with natural sustainable and renewable resources for generations to come. To help ensure that the rainforests are preserved, here are some things you can do:

1. Plant trees and plants, and encourage reforestation (the replanting of trees in former forests).

2. Visit parks that protect rainforests and wildlife.

3. Support sustainable and ecologically harvested rainforest products such as nuts, fruits, and medicinal plants.

4. Choose "certified rainforest-safe" wood products from sustainably managed forests.

5. Avoid products made from wild animals and their skins.

6. Select "captive-bred" rather than exotic "wild-caught" pets that have been collected from the wild.

7. Follow the "Three R" rule—reduce, reuse, and recycle. Reduce your waste by buying less and by buying products with as little packaging as possible. Individual packaging generates more waste than bulk packaging. Use reusable products rather than disposable ones. Recycle paper, plastic, aluminum, glass, and other materials, and buy recycled paper and products.

8. Conserve water by only using what you need and not letting taps run.

9. Endorse eco-friendly companies.

10. Read books about rainforests and rainforest conservation.

11. Get involved by volunteering and sharing with others your knowledge about preserving the rainforests and their plants and animals.